IS GRANDMA
A WITCH?

CONSTANCE DELL

This book is a public forgiveness to my mother for giving me an inferiority complex that I've lived with most of my life.

1955 was a major year in our life. I graduated from high school and got married the same week. In November, we had our first son. In August, the largest hurricane came roaring up the East Coast of the United States. The major news magazines said it was the largest in recorded history, doing great damage along the coast and to the national Appalachian Trail.

Its name was "CONNIE"

Dedication

To my Lord and Savior, Jesus Christ.

To my sweet husband whose support got stronger as this fiasco of my childhood went on.

Also to my four children: two boys and two girls and my ten grandchildren: three boys and seven girls.

Special thanks to my grandson - Roy, for all his computer skills.

Also another special thanks to our son Michael for all the editing, formatting, cover and special effects in this book.

Finally, it is dedicated to myself for the therapy that I've needed for the last sixty years.

Quotes That Inspired Me

"To live, to struggle, to be in love with life - in love with all life holds, joyful or sorrowful - in fulfillment the fullness of life is open to all."

Betty Smith – author of a Tree Grows in Brooklyn

"To have a child, to plant a tree, to write a book, that he said was a full life."

Emile Zola – First Nobel Prize winner in Literature, 1901

"I have finally done all the three things, and I can honestly say I've had a full life, a good life, a nice life; I am at peace with myself and the world."

Constance Dell

Prologue

My mother was a witch...No really I'm not kidding. You don't believe me?

She was the seventh daughter, of a seventh son.

This made my grandfather a warlock, or a male witch.

I'm the seventh daughter of a seventh daughter.

So what does that make me?

Chapter 1 - Parade

I would inevitably lose at least two pairs of mittens every winter. At the start of winter I would pray, "Dear God, please don't let me lose my mittens this year."

In the middle of winter, I would pray, "Dear God, please help me find my mittens." It was like the poem of the Three Little Kittens:

Three little kittens lost their mittens

And they began to cry----

O mommy dear, look here, look here

Our mittens we have lost

Lost your mittens?

You naughty kittens ----

Now you shall have no pie!

The three little kittens found their mittens

And they began to sigh ----

O mommy dear look here, look here

Our mittens we have found

Found your mittens?

You sweet little kittens

Wash them and hang them out to dry

And you shall have some pie----"

The point of all this, was my mother was like the first mother cat but, certainly not like the last. When I would lose my mittens-- her stare was as cold as my little hands. They stayed that way until I found my mittens.

I was born on November 22, 1934, and that date happened to be our Thanksgiving Day every year until 1941 when President Franklin Delano Roosevelt made it officially the last Thursday in November.

I was so glad, as I could have my birthday on my day instead of my mother's day out.

You see every Thanksgiving we would go downtown to Woodward Avenue to see the Detroit Christmas parade. We would see Santa get the key to all the little girls' and boys' hearts in Detroit in front of the J.L. Hudson department store.

Then we would walk over to Greenfield's cafeteria for lunch and then to the Fox theater for a movie.

All this is without mittens and with frost bitten hands. So I was glad that mother no longer had a birthday excuse to go to the parade.

I didn't know what a thanksgiving turkey dinner was until many years later.

Once I asked my mother where she got my name. There was a beautiful movie star by the name of Constance Bennett, so I was hoping that was the answer.

Instead she said she knew, "I was going to be constantly in trouble." For the most part, she was right.

Me, 1935 – 6-7months old

Chapter 2 - My Childhood

I spent most of my childhood alone. I would go down stairs into the basement after dinner and play "school" until bedtime.

I had a little room about six feet by eight feet that had been a coal bin. When we switched to a gas furnace, my dad cleaned it up and painted the room white. I had a piece of slate with the corner broken off for a black board. My dolls were my pupils and I loved teaching them English. I think I wanted to be an English teacher.

At this time, we had moved into the back half of the house. We rented the front half to the Fleshers. A nice middle age couple with no children, so that apartment was fine for them. It only had one bed room, which had been my parents' room, before they took ours, mine and Mary's room in the back apartment. We moved down stairs to Ralph's room since he had gotten married.

Mrs Flesher was a real nice lady. She stayed home and was a "house wife". She was so nice to me. I guess I was the child she never had. We would bake cookies together and she would read to me. My mother didn't care; she got rid of me for a while.

When we got ready to move to Canada (the first time to live there) she gave me her white lamb cookie jar to remember her by. It was where we put the cookies we made.

I kept that cookie jar even into my marriage didn't know what happened to it. Sometimes, not too often, I see a white lamb cookie jar in an antique shop, and I think back to Mrs Flesher. The lady I wanted to be my mother.

During this time, I had two girlfriends. They both had the same first name.

Rose Marie Fisher was age ten and a little worldlier than I. She lived in an upstairs flat on the corner of the next street that ended at my street. Her mother worked and her older brother took care of her, when he was around.

We played different games then Rosie Babberski and I played. Rosie lived on the street right before mine, right opposite Hunter Elementary.

The school was rather a unique school because it had an outside fire escape. It was a long wide steel tube from the second floor to the ground.

There was a door that locked from the inside in one of the rooms. There were two little holes at the top of the escape that let in a little light from outside. I called them fairy lights.

On the week-ends, the neighborhood kids used to play in the tube. We would climb inside and crawl up to the top and slide down. Screaming loudly and making a lot of noise. It was great fun and all the kids loved it.

Back in the day, we all had to take a musical instrument. I chose the violin. My mother didn't quite like my choice.

She would put me in the glassed in porch. Close the door to the house, and proceeded to run the vacuum cleaner inside the house while I practiced. Needless to say when we moved to Canada we left the violin behind.

Rosie was my age, seven or seven and a half. Rosie and I played with dolls under her back porch, which was held up with posts along the outside wall and at the corner.

Also under the porch was the basement door. We had our play house under the porch and Rosie's grandpa spent his time in the basement or cellar as they called them. We would sit on his lap and he would give us pennies.

One day I went over and called Rosie to come out and play. She wasn't home, but grandpa was. He said come down to the cellar, which we had done hundreds of times. So I did and I was sitting on his lap, when he offered me a penny, as I looked down to take it, he had his male member out of his pants. I hadn't ever seen one of those things, and I was kind of sacred. So I told him I had to go home, my mother would be looking for me. I jumped off his lap and ran out of the cellar, out of the play house under the porch, across the back yard to the alley gate got home as fast as I could. I had left my penny behind.

Somewhere during the Detroit years, my mother took a job at Ternstedt's on the corner of Fort and Livernois in Detroit. Fisher Body was the premier division of General Motors.

During world WW11, Fisher Body built the M4A3 Sherman Tank that was used in the Battle of the Bulge in December of 1944.

The M4A3 was armed with a 75MM cannon. There were 1,711 M4A3's built between February to September in 1944.

Ternstedt remained at 6307 W. Fort Street Detroit until it moved and became G.M. Warren.

Mother was possibly part of the "Rosie the Riveter" movement at the time. Rosie was the star of a government campaign aimed at recruiting female workers for munitions plants during the war. It became a famous Icon.

The American women entered the workforce in unprecedented numbers during WW11 as male enlistments left gaping holes in the industrial labor force between 1940 and 1945.

By 1945 nearly one out of every four married women worked outside the home in factories and shipyards.

There was a documentary film in 1980 titled, "The Life and Times of Rosie the Riveter."

This was the beginning of women wearing men's pants, slacks as they are known, and working right along with the men. It was possibly the end of the "stay at home" housewife who left her dress and heels at home to dawn a neck scarf around her head, put on her slacks, grab her lunch pail and head for work.

It was possibly the beginning of life as we know it. Both parents are working, two cars in the garage, driving to day care, dropping off kids at school, going to the office. Later go and pick up something for dinner. Everyone is helping out with family chores and everyone doing their own thing.

The Sparr family, Brenda's holding me and Mary's holding her Shirley Temple doll.

Chapter 3 - Goodbye America

As I said before my name is Constance Spar and I was born in Detroit Michigan on November 1934. I was born with a Caul, or what my mother called a veil, as it covered my face.

A caul is part of the amniotic- membrane occasionally found on a child's head and face at birth. They are very rare only one in eighty thousand. They are supposed to protect the baby from ever drowning. An infant born with a Caul was supposed to mean that I was set apart to do great things in the world which I haven't done so far.

My mother sent the veil to uncle Harry in England, as there was a superstition that any sailor with a Caul, while he was aboard the ship it wouldn't sink.

My Uncle Harry wore it for the rest of his navy life when he disembarked for the last time taking the Caul with him. The ship left port; it was hit by a torpedo and sank.

Uncle Harry was a good old boy he loved a party. Well the story goes that one Wednesday evening grandfather and his brood were coming back from prayer meeting. They got to the top of the hill. They saw their house. It looked like the attic was on fire, they ran like crazy to the house, went in the door up the many steps to the third floor attic threw open the door and there sat and stood twenty drunken sailors. All with a beer in their hands, and every empty bottle had a lite candle in it.

I went to Hunter Elementary School from kindergarten to about third grade. Somewhere between second and fourth grade around 1942 to 1944 in the summer my parents moved to Canada.

I kind of remember moving day as that was the day that older boys trapped me between two garages and a wooden fence that hid the alley and tried to become my new best friends.

As scared as I was of them, I was also scared that the moving truck that was parked in the front of my house would leave without me, but that didn't happen. My folks didn't leave without me, and so I sat in the backseat of my dad's Chevy with my cat Mickey on my lap.

My deceased sister's headstone is in the trunk. It was there because Woodmere Cemetery wouldn't accept it; it was a soft stone and couldn't take the cold Michigan winters.

My folks couldn't leave it in the basement of our house in Oakwood. So they took it with them to Leamington Canada.

We went to the big old cobble stone house, with the veranda that ran across the front.

This was my introduction to "Breeze In" that would eventuality become a Tourist Home or B&B as it is known now.

We buried Emmy's headstone in the back of "Breeze In". Two other graves would join her later.

Chapter 4 - Big Brother (Mutt and Jeff)

When I was born, Ralph came upstairs from his basement bedroom. He asked my dad "what did mother have?" A girl answered dad, to which Ralph replied "Oh another one of those". He turned around and went back to his room.

Through the years as I grew up, I found out there were seven years difference in my two older sisters. There was six years difference between Mary and .myself. Nineteen years between Ralph and I. Needless to say we didn't much in common.

The spring before we left Oakwood my brother graduated Wayne in the first Masters Degree course ever .Wayne was in Detroit. It wasn't "Wayne Collage", "Wayne University" or "Wayne State" as it is now. It was just plain Wayne!

The day everyone was preparing for his graduation party and was busy running around, I decided to cut my bangs, probably because I wasn't getting any attention.

So when my mother saw my chopped up hair she asked, "Why did you do this?" I answered "so I could see out". My mother was getting ready to spank the pants off me.

Ralph came out of the house and picked me up, said to mother "don't spank her, she's cute"! My brother became my hero that day! He was really my big brother. We were always together, when he wasn't at work at the pharmacy. We were like Mutt and Jeff.

As time went on Ralph got engaged to Phyllis, the niece of Mayor Cobo of Detroit, she was a debutante, was somewhere in the early forties.

As the wedding was being planned, Ralph told my parents that Phyllis didn't want children at the wedding. My dad told him, if his Lassie (who was me) wasn't going to the wedding, neither was he.

Later Ralph said that I had to be well mannered and behave myself. Now this opened the situation that if I came, than Phyllis's bratty twin nephews would also have to be included.

Now the wedding was a great big affair. The reception was held at the "Le Plaza Hotel" on West Grand Boulevard in downtown Detroit.

The banquet room had two sets of French doors that a joined the hall and the banquet room, the nephews spent the whole evening running and screaming and making a figure eight pattern in and out of the French doors.

I on the other hand was the most behaved eight years old in history. I spent the night standing on a lot of men's shoes dancing the night away. I even danced with Mayor Cobo himself.

Ralph was so proud of me, our bond became stronger. We kept in touch through our adult lives.

Then on October the first, twenty thousand fourteen Ralph Spar died. He was six months from his one hundredth birthday. I loved my only big brother.

I miss him.

Dr. Ralph Spar 1949

Chapter 5 - Bonny Brenda

Brenda was the sweetest person on earth. In her older years, when I was in my early to late twenties, she was somewhere in her thirties to forties. She would see someone that needed help and she would go to them and help them. Even to the length of getting into their families and helping out. I don't mean not like a busy body. I mean she would ask how she could help and she would.

If they were British, watch out. She would bring them home with her and find agencies that would help them. Meanwhile she would keep them at her home and care for them.

When Brenda was a teenager my mother would meet her coming home from school.

Mother would say "here take her; I can't stand another minute of her."

The "her" she was talking about was me. She would put me in the buggy and wheel me down to the corner, met the bus, take Brenda's books and hand the buggy over to her.

Brenda was my second mother and remained that all her life. Thank God!

Brenda had a rough life also from mother. When my mother was younger and before I was born my two sisters and mother shopped together and did a few things together. Things changed when I came along - Sorry!

When Brenda was asked to her senior prom she got a new dress and shoes and got everything ready for her big night.

But she must have done something that mother didn't like. Mother just waited.

Prom night came; Brenda was beautiful in her dress. The young man came to the house to pick her up. Mother let him in, took the flowers, and called Brenda to say he was here.

Brenda came into the room looking lovely, all excited, and happy, then mother gave the flowers back to the young man and told him Brenda wasn't going that evening. Mother gets even.

The poor guy! Poor Brenda ran into her room broken-hearted and in tears

Brenda did graduate that year. Soon after she married the man across the street, which was thirteen to fifteen years older than her, we never did find out his age.

Her story gets worse, thanks to mother. Our sweet dad felt really bad about Brenda's whole life.

Brenda wanted dad to give her away at her wedding. Nothing would have made daddy happier, even with the difference in age. But mother told dad that he was not to go near the church, much less in it.

Now you have to remember dad was between a rock and a hard place. He had two other daughters at home that he had to protect as best he could.

He was told that on her wedding day Brenda stood out on the sidewalk in her wedding gown holding her flowers waiting for him. She thought for sure he would come.

She stood there crying until the minister came out and told her it was past time, and she really had to come inside.

When Brenda had her first little girl, Bonnie, she would cover her up when they came out of the house, as we lived right across the street.

If mother wouldn't let dad come to the wedding, then mother wasn't going to see her first grand daughter. That was sad but true.

As I got older and married and had my own children, Brenda and I kept in touch. She still lived in California and I lived in Michigan. They would come to Detroit to see Zee's family and also come to see my family.

I found out that Zee had been married before and it was annulled by the girl's family.

There was a little girl from that union, which made me her step aunt. So I had a niece who was older than me.

When Brenda died of cancer on November 19, 1985, I was there to say "Good Bye" My only request was that her girls wouldn't bury her on my birthday, November 22nd, which they didn't.

Brenda died the same date as my mother on English time. Actually mother died

November 19, 1979. With the time difference in England it turned out to be the same day.

I loved her as my second mother. As they say "The Good Die Young"

Chapter 6 - Sweet Little Emmy

I didn't know how old my sister Emmy was when she was killed by a drunk driver on Fort Street. I wasn't born yet. It happened right in front of the house.

There was a Cadillac dealer on Fort Street. When he heard of the accident he took one of his new caddy's and put Emmy in the back seat, blood and all, drove mother and her to the nearest hospital.

My mother was so thankful that she sold eight new cars for him. She told her friends, neighbors and did everything except take out an advertisement in the Detroit News.

Mother had a stillbirth before Emmy was born. After Emmy passed away she had another stillbirth. A stillbirth is a baby that

¹⁵ born, but is too small or frail to survive. There is a birth and a death certificate.

After Emmy was killed, they moved to Oakwood. I was told they had an old boat dragged up from the Rouge River to a vacant lot where dad converted it into a front and back duplex. I don't know if the boat part was true; that just what I was told.

Mother was pregnant with Mary. Mary's story is a story in itself. Six years later I came along quite unexpected and unwanted. That's how I became the seventh daughter of a seventh daughter.

I found this out when I was nearly fifty.

Chapter 7 - Sister Mary

Mary was six years older than me, Brenda was eighteen, Mary was eleven and I was five.

That broke the chain of the "Elephant Woman", who my mother called herself, as she had a child every seven years, like an elephant so she said.

Now again, Mary's story is in part she told me later as I wasn't around for the first six years.

My folks had been going to Leamington for years even before Mary was born.

Mary had infantile paralysis or polio (as it is known today) at a very early age.

There was another girl in Oakwood who had polio also. Mother and Mary would go to a clinic in Detroit with this girl, her mother and her dad. Her dad had a car and would drive into Detroit.

Both girls' parents were told that the girls would never walk. They would be in a wheelchair for the rest of their lives.

My mother was a great believer of massage, she would take Mary down to lake Erie with an ironing board and some massage oil, She would lay Mary on the board ,massage her with oil, in the sun. Every time Mary pulled her legs up, mother would spank her. Mary would cry and stretch and mother would massage them.

People would ask mother what was wrong with her child; Mother, with her deep British brogue, wouldn't answer them.

She pretended that she was foreign and didn't understand. So they stopped asking.

I do remember Mary being in a heavy leg brace. We slept in the same bed. At night

Mary would throw her leg, the one with the cast over mine, and wake me up.

We slept in the same downstairs bedroom that Ralph had when he was home.

Mary and mother seemed to get along better than the rest of us. Later on when we were both older I remember dad bringing Mary down to "Breeze In" on Friday night for the weekend and taking her back to Detroit on Monday morning - Early !

She would go to Commerce High School and dad would go to work. Mary was able to walk. She had a slight limp when she got tired. Otherwise she did pretty well.

After Mary graduated she became the first one in our family to fly. She flew away to California as soon as she could, to live with Brenda.

She married Zee's nephew James We all went to California for the wedding.

Not by plane or train, we went by greyhound bus. I was around fourteen at the time. The bus was full of young sailors. But that is another story.

Chapter 8 - Popsie (That's Me)

I didn't remember going to the Lighthouse Campground in Leamington, as I was just a baby and then a small child, through the years at the Lighthouse Campground.

However, I was told everyone called me "Popsie". I guess because I was always popping up.

I used to go down the small hill to the beach and pick up everyone's shoes.

I would bring them back to our cabin, put them on the front step, in pairs and sell them back to their owners for a penny a piece.

They must have expected it, as they always had pennies. Even then I was resourceful at the age of four or five. We went to Leamington every summer for years before my parents actually bought the property there.

Chapter 9 - My Grandfather - Man of The World

Grandfather, Thomas Holder became a widower after the birth of Beatrice, his eighth child. So the children grew up without a mother. That may explain why my mother was the way she was. I knew I never wanted to be that kind of mother. I wanted to love my children and have them love me.

The eight children, two boys and six girls all went to private boarding schools by train.

In the summer, when they were all home, the housekeeper would come out in the early evening and call "Ethel, Alice, Thomas, Carry, Harry, Adea, Ruth, and Beatrice, come in for supper".

My mother would tell that story over and over. She would rattle those names off like she was a train conductor.

Grandfather was an auctioneer, which is probably where I got the gift of gab, as they say.

Grandfather also had two stores in Morecome Bay. One day he told his employee to put the black blouses on sale and put a sign in the window.

The next morning he came to the store and was met possibly, by the first picket line in the history of Morecame Bay ever.

The employee had done her job. She did what she was told she had printed a sign.

BLACK LADIES' BLOUSES

FOR SALE----50% OFF

The ladies of the community had made a circle in front of the door of the store in protest!

Grandpa Holden 1913

Chapter 10 - Abracadabra

My mother had a crystal ball. She kept it in a purple satin box when she wasn't using it to read her clients' fortunes.

She also read tea leaves, palms, and bumps on the side of the head. She never went in for tarot cards. She said those were for beginners.

Mother had been "Madam Ruth" during the depression. She made extra money doing readings especially when she would go to the parties given by Mayor Cobo of Detroit. She would be a special attraction for his guests. This also gave her clients for her private readings at home in Oakwood.

After we moved to Leamington mother had séances on Thursday nights. I would be sent to my room.

One night I snuck down the stairs, Close to the top. I would sit and stick my small face between the spindles

There were people sitting around a card table with their hands on top. **Now that table did rise.** I have to admit it wasn't high, But it did rise.

I sat there with wide eyes and an open mouth. My mother's head turned around and she caught me out of corner of her eye. She rose from her chair, came to the bottom of the stairs. Her dark eyes staring right through me, she waved her finger then her hand and said, "If I can do that to the table, what can I do to you?

Chapter 11 - Santa Claus Isn't Coming To Town

I was about fourteen or fifteen when I was down on my hands and knees washing the kitchen floor in the apartment over the garage. A flat as they called it then.

My mother was sitting in an easy chair smoking her cigarette looking like Queen Victoria. She kept telling me to touch up the corner that wasn't clean enough.

After doing it over five or six times, I got mad, squeezed the scrub cloth out, and threw it at her. I said to her "If it's not good enough do it yourself."

She glared at me and I swear my mother made up this famous saying, as I had never heard it before. She said, "I don't get mad I get even" She did!

That Christmas, I got four 78 RPN records, but no record player needless to say, I was crying. I looked at my dad; he had tears in his eyes.

My mother had once told me that I was my father's big mistake! Mother said I was just the gleam in my father's eye.

I guess I was. It remained that way. I was his Lassie and he was my daddy. We loved each other and got along great.

After the Christmas adventure was over, I was not allowed to take my records out of the house. There were a few times when mother was gone, that daddy would say "take your records and go to Mary's house". My friend just lived down the street. "Be sure to be back before your mother gets home". That was the beginning of my learning to be sneaky!

Chapter 12 - "Go west Young Man" No go east!

One Saturday night my friends and I were going to go to Windsor to the show. My friends, the few I had were somewhat used to my mother's quirks.

She took a hold of the boy's hand that was going to drive. She looked at him very seriously and said "don't go to Windsor; go to the other way toward Wheatley."

He decided that maybe we should go to Wheatley. Then we all decided just to stay in Leamington.

Every Sunday morning my dad had a ritual. He would wake up make coffee, and turn on the radio to hear the weather and the road conditions as he had to drive back to Detroit to go to work.

That morning the first report he heard was that there was an eight car pile pile up on highway three at seven P.M. last night. That's about when we would be near Windsor. Mother's palm reading was right on again!

There was a period in my young life that I don't remember all the facts too well. Maybe I have blocked them out. Or maybe just chose to forget, but as far as I can recall, I must have been from thirteen to fifteen at the time.

My mother went away for several weeks, even months. I never knew where or why. I think she may have had a nervous breakdown or something.

But what I do remember vividly that it was around Christmas, My dad had gone to "Puce Ontario" to see who I called Uncle Frank and Aunt Ida. They weren't my uncle and aunt, but I didn't have any, so they were my adopted ones

I was left alone in Leamington perhaps with Mrs "B". I don't really remember. But what I remember was sitting with my then boyfriend Bob at his house on the floor of their living room, looking up at their high Christmas tree, crying my eyes out, feeling extremely sad, being left at Christmas.

It is even hard to think and write about it even now some sixty years later.

Gentiles Only   No Pets Allowed

"HOME FROM HOME"
PHONE LEAMINGTON *1511 m*

Breeze In

COTTAGES, CABINS & ROOMS
● Reasonable Rates

SEACLIFF PARK
LEAMINGTON - ONTARIO - CANADA

W. & R. SPURR, Props.   (Over)

Breeze In and the flat next door

The first four cabins

Chapter 13 - Pal

One day a black semi-long body and kind of tall legged dog, a small husky maybe, walked into our lives. He took to my dad right away. My dad took to him too. It was a mutual admiration society. Dad named him Pal.

They would do everything together. Pal would lie down while dad worked on the cabins. If dad moved from the site, Pal moved with him. They were inseparable.

Dad used to drive around the park from our side to Park Street to where our cabins were. Pal would go with him. Than one day he wouldn't get in the car. He took off running across the park. So dad got in the car and drove around the park. When he got to the park gates, there was Pal sitting waiting for him.

So it was! Every time dad would get in the car and tell Pal" going to the cabins", Pal would take off and cross the park before dad even got there. He'd sit at the gate waiting for him.

This ritual went on for years Pal takes off Dad leaves Pal meets dad at the gates and runs alongside of the car, the short trip down Park Street to the cabins. Both arrived at the same time.

Well this one morning dad told Pal he was going and Pal took off. When dad got to the top of the park at highway 10, there was an army convoy of jeeps going down the road.

Dad waited for them to pass which took a few minutes. Finally dad turned onto highway 10, down the block to Park Street and down to the park gates.

Pal was getting antsy and he was dancing around with excitement when he saw dad coming he was so thrilled that he jumped in front of the car and daddy hit him.

Pal was dead instantly. Daddy stopped the car, picked Pal up and put him in the backseat. He drove home with blood on his hands and tears in his eyes.

When he got home, he told mother that he had killed Pal, his beloved dog, his best friend in the world.

My mother said "good I never liked that dog anyway." Daddy and I buried pal next to Mickey the cat in the back of Breeze In. We both cried.

Chapter 14 - Leamington, Ontario, Canada

"A swinging Town"

We lived across from Seacliff Park. Back when it was the greatest place on earth.

The big name bands came to play at the outside band shell of the Sea Cliff Pavilion. It had a second porch all around the building, a great place to sneak in to see the bands.

They had some big headliners of the day Gene Krupa, Harry James, Ralph Flanagan, Benny Goodman, Jimmy and Tommy Dorsey and of course the one and only "In the Mood", Glen Miller.

It was so much fun running around the park at night dancing outside of the dance floor. We couldn't afford to go in, but we were having the time of our lives.

My mother didn't know where I was, or could care less. But I'm sure she knew where the music was I was there.

That summer I met a girl a little older than me in the park one night, She was about eighteen I have forgotten her name, but I think it was Audrey.

Audrey taught me a lot for my young age. I was in my early teens and eager to learn!

Audrey and I started hanging out together. My mother knew nothing about Audrey. She would have done bodily harm to me if she had known.

Audrey taught me how to smoke although we didn't inhale. We would stand across from each other on the toilet seat at the pavilion. So no one could see our feet and we would drop our cigarettes into the toilet water.

I would take a drag on the cigarette, blow out the smoke, and cough; I did this several times until I mastered it. Hurrah!

I've mastered my first addiction. We met some older guys and would hang out with them in the park. We danced, talked, smoked and made out, like hand holding and a little kissing. It was all very new to me but when the pocket flask came out, it was new to me also. I had a very strange sense about it and left before I got into more trouble.

When I think back on it now, that would have been a very bad scene. This was the same park that as a younger child I would crash all the church picnics, Baptist, Lutheran, Methodist, Presbyterian, you name it.

I would be baptized in Lake Erie with each group. So there was quite a contrast in my activities at the park.

After the Audrey part of my young life, I decided to try and stay out of trouble. From then on I spent my time diving off the Leamington dock, over the piling from the break wall. That wasn't too smart either, as you had to dive past the piling to hit the water. I was the only girl to do that.

I'd go swimming off the beach in Lake Erie. My Mickey cat would follow me any place I went. He thought he was a dog. While I was swimming, Mickey would walk back and forth in the surf, as it hit the sand. He would shake his paws with each step. I always thought cats didn't like water. That shows what I knew.

Swimming in Lake Erie was wonderful, delightful, exciting. When your way out there in the water over your head and very deep you have such a sense of freedom.

It isn't until you start thinking of where you are and how deep it is that you get scared (I guess I forgot that I was born with a veil). Then you panic and you turn around and swim like hell toward the shore.

You know, I always had a dream to swim the English Channel. My mother said that it was too expensive. You had to have boats, spotters, be all greased up etc. She said "besides you couldn't do it. I didn't do it. But I sure would have liked to have given it a try.

People have told me, I should put it on my bucket list. But at my age the bucket is pretty rusty. Also during that summer a guy named Bob, whose family had been coming to our cabins from Detroit for years, came down with a friend of his named Mike Dell.

Mike and Bob drove down from Detroit in Mike's car to see me. I had gone around with Bob when his family spent two weeks every year here. We were friends nothing serious.

I had a girlfriend named Joan, who spent the summer here from Detroit. It all worked out nice. I paired up with Mike, and Bob and Joan got together. Mike was in the U.S. Navy at the time. He was due to ship out to Kwajalein an island in the Marshall Islands in the Pacific Ocean.

Mike came down to Leamington a few more times to see me that summer. The first time he came back I took him to meet a couple of my friends (who were boys).

When he met Johnny the blacksmith's son, he was told, "Never let her drive your car" "Why?" asked Mike. "Because", said Johnny, "she'll drop your transmission".

After that we went to see Elwood whose father owned the local gas station. Elwood was at the gas station working on his own car. He looked up and saw us coming. We talked for a little bit and Elwood said to Mike "I'm working on my car don't ever let her drive your car". Mike responded "I understand". We said goodbye and left him working on his transmission.

On our second date I wasn't so hard on him. He had passed the test. He was still cute and cool in his uniform.

On that date we drove to Point Pelee. Back then you could drive to where the road hit the sand. You could get out of your car walk through the sand to the point, the most southern part in Canada, when Canadians go south for the winter. They don't go to Point Pelee. They go to Florida like the rest of us.

At the point the water comes in from both sides of the beach. It has a very bad undertow and is a very dangerous place to swim. So you pick one side or the other to swim. One side is usually rougher than the other. Depending on how you want to swim, you take your pick. The point is now part of the Canadian National Park Service.

They have an information center and a museum. You get on a tram and go out the very same road to the very same spot. But now it's a parking lot for the trams to arrive and exit which is better for the environment but not so much fun for the young people.

Compared to when we were young we would all put in a quarter for gas and drive to the point. As crazy kids we went off road (in a non-off road vehicle) through trees and bushes, roots, and bumps with or without lights. Not too smart, but fun.

After the trip to the point Mike and I went to Leamington. As you come into town from the highway there is a giant red tomato, right at the tip of two roads.

If you were there at the right time you could get a free 6 oz can of chilled Heinz tomato juice.

When we were going somewhere, we would say "meet you at the tomato". The H. J. Heinz Company in Leamington was the second largest Heinz plant in the world.

Most people who live in Leamington worked at Heinz Factory, or grew tomatoes for Heinz. They made it all ketchup, tomato products, and my favorite pickles-both sweet and dill.

Mike took me to Diana Sweets for sundaes. The first time we went Mike made friends for life with the waitresses. We had our Sundaes; the bill was two dollars, now Mike being in a U. S. Navy uniform left a five dollar tip.

The next time we were there the waitresses were tripping over each other to wait on us. It was the best place for ice cream and the best place for Mike's ego. He loved to go there, and we went every time he came to Leamington to see me.

Now I think (after about sixty-five years) it has changed its name to "Sweet Retreat". But either way it was a good place to be.

Mike and I only saw each other when Mike got a leave. We wrote to each other, letters not texts. I kind of liked him and I think he liked me, but you know what they say about sailors having a girl in every port.

Fall came and I started Leamington High, I had a lot to occupy my mind.

Chapter 15 - Ho Ho, Away They Go!

Sometime I felt like humpty dumpty, who was so broken that not even the king's horses or all the king's men couldn't put me together again.

During that fall my mother got the bright idea that her and daddy should go back to England, as they hadn't been back since coming to America.

Daddy liked the idea and said we should take Constance with us. It would be more invaluable than six months of school.

My mother said "No I want to have fun, not drag a kid around with us all the time". But years later she took Ralph's son to England.

So it was decided that I would move back into Breeze In, into my old room, with a window facing the flat.

I moved from my curtained off roll away bed, that was alongside of the twin cement laundry tubs and my dad's car in the garage under the flat, into the main house.

There was a family by the name Bullnard renting Breeze In at the time. My mother apparently had made some kind of a deal with the Bullnards for me to live with them for the next four months or so.

The Bullnards had an only daughter whose name was Barbara or BB for short. She was eighteen and out of school, kind of engaged to a fellow in the service. He would come home every second weekend. On Friday night very late he would come to see BB first, then go home.

Now, Barbara hated me. She hated the fact that I was living with them. I was not allowed to call her BB. It had to be Barbara.

Her mother had a set of colored dinner dishes. Barbara would set the table with the three of them with multicolored plates and cups. My place would be set in dark blue. It was just little subtle things that told me, I had better know my place.

One evening I was coming down the stairs for dinner. Barbara and her mother were in the kitchen, BB was complaining about me living with them. Her mother said "how would you feel living with people you hardly knew for months?" "She's just a poor little rich girl." To which Barbara replied "I'd give it a try."

I stood on the stairs in shock. Me a rich girl?, I never knew that ! I turned around and went back upstairs.

There was no television back then, so I spent a lot of time in my room looking at the empty flat next door, with tears in my eyes.

Chapter 16 - One Fish, Two Fish, Red Fish, Blue Fish

When my parents finally came back from England, bringing me Andy Mcnab, a Scottish highlander doll, complete with bagpipes, black cap and coat, a kilt of red, black and white plaid. I fell in love with him immediately. I still have him today, one of the good memories of my childhood.

Another thing they brought back was brochures on commercial stainless steel fryers for fish and chips.

They had decided to build and operate an English fish and chip shop. We had seven or eight cabins and two winterized houses on Park Street, on the other side of Sea Cliff. There was still some land left to build a restaurant.

My parents spent all winter on blueprints, plans, suppliers, and contractors. Everything they needed for construction and going into business.

Very early in the spring they started construction on what was referred to as the fish shop.

It went up rather quickly and the gleaming stainless steel deep fryer came all the way from Bonnie England.

My mother put an advertisement in the newspaper that Spar's Fish and Chips would be giving away free dinners, if you could stand the smoke. Being new the equipment would smoke until the newness wore off.

It was the biggest thing to hit Leamington in years. We made over two hundred dinners by the time we were done. After the free dinners we had our grand opening. We were full every night and Fridays were standing room only.

My dad was the cook. He would prepare the fish and chips. The fish came from Halifax, Nova Scotia. The fish was at least 6 feet, 500 pounds, descaled with no head or tail. Dad would cut it lengthwise. We would help him open the fish to its full width-wise. He would measure and mark in 4 inches x 4 inches x1 inch. This was second nature to him because after all he was a tool and die machinist who was used to using a micrometer.

The halibut is the largest of the flat fish; they grow to seven or eight feet long and up to 700 pounds.

Then came the potato peeler. It was a cylinder on legs with a crank. He'd put in ten pounds of potatoes and turn the crank and the potatoes would jump around and get peeled.

Back then nothing was electrical. I guess the potato peeler could have been motorized, but it wasn't, so dad had a hard job in cranking it. I tried it, but it was much too hard for me.

There was a couple hours start up time each day and at least an hour clean up each night.

Mother took care of the register and counter. I was the waitress on the booths. We were open from four pm to nine pm on the weekdays. Three pm to eight pm on Saturdays and closed on Sundays.

I was sixteen that summer. I met a lot of nice young men on the job and got great tips, which were all mine. Life seemed to finally be going well. Until!

Chapter 17 - The Letter

Then came the letter. I think it may have been the biggest shock of my poor dad's life.

He had retired and moved to Canada after working over twenty years in the states. He had put into Social Security, Which was just forming at the time. But the first year was an organizational year and it didn't count toward the twenty years needed for benefits.

Daddy had to go back to Michigan, get a job, and work one more year to be eligible.

So here again they were going and leaving me behind like before, as I had to finish the school year.

This time they got an old friend a literal old lady, whom we knew for years. Mrs Buchanan came and lived with me in the flat.

She was a sweet old lady. She was also Billy's grandmother. Billy and I used to play store together in the foundation of "Row Inn" that had burned down when we were kids.

That's another long story, so to keep it simple. We owned another house next to "Breeze In". It had burned down and in its place daddy built four cabins. That started our summer cabin business in the first place.

Now getting back to living with Mrs B in the flat I continued go to Leamington High. Mother and dad moved to River Rouge Michigan to stay with friends until they could find a little place to live until dad put in his year.

They stayed in River Rouge for a while. I would come over to Detroit some week-ends. I remember this one winter week-end when I was at River Rouge and Mike was home on leave.

He came to get me to go out for the evening. We hadn't seen each other for a while, but we wrote all the time.

As the evening was coming to a close, Mike was putting something in his car. Back then they had a latch that was in the lid of the trunk. To make a long story short, the lid came down, as Mike was looking in the trunk, right on top of his head.

Mike's head bled red all over his white uniform. It wouldn't stop. Our friend that lived in the house put a clean soft rug around his head and rushed him to the nearest hospital. They stitched him up, gave him some pills and sent him home. That's exactly what he did. He drove home alone.

Dad got a job at Great Lakes Shipping down river. He was a tool and die maker.

He stayed at the shipyard long enough to build one of the biggest ship ever built by that company.

Meanwhile they moved into a little house on Victoria Avenue behind the Security Bank on Fort Street in Lincoln Park.

I continued to go to school and live with Mrs B in the flat. I would see my parents a couple of week-ends a month until they moved to Lincoln Park Michigan.

I was still only sixteen years of age, traveling back and forth between two countries. Diplomatic Ambassador!

Chapter 18 - Hi, Ho, Hi, Ho, Off to Work I Go!

Mother and dad had moved into Lincoln Park and the place was TINY, not small but tiny. It had a living room, bedroom, kitchen and bath.

I had finished tenth grade when daddy said he wanted me with them not living in Canada, so when school was over for summer, I moved back to the U.S.A again.

I slept on a hide-a-way bed in the living room. My mother decided that since I would be seventeen that winter. I might as well get used to working (Like I hadn't been doing, since I was fourteen.)

Mother had a friend who was the Personnel Director at Ferry Morse Seed Company on Brush Street in Detroit. I was hired in as summer began as a file clerk. I thought that I would return to school in the fall.

Well, mother had other plans for me. She told me that on my way home from work; instead of coming home I could get off the streetcar at Southwestern High School, right on Fort Street, and go to night school.

Now Constance M. Spar was working eight hours a day and going to night school three hours three nights a week.

So it was – I'd catch the streetcar at nine p. m. After school, get home a little before ten p. m. Go to bed; get up the next morning early, to be at work at nine a. m.

I did this for about two years. Now, all during this time of turmoil Mike was still in and out of my life with letters and leaves. He never knew where to send the letters or where to come when on leave, as he never knew for sure where I was. I could have been in Leamington, Canada or Lincoln Park, Michigan.

I continued to work at the seed company and on Friday nights after work I would take the Greyhound Bus from Windsor to Leamington after going through the Detroit Windsor Tunnel on the tunnel bus.

The Greyhound was great as it would let me off on highway 10 right on top of Seacliff Park. That only left me with a short gravel road to walk down to Breeze In, the cabins and a little further Lake Erie.

I'd spend another week-end and return to Lincoln Park on Sunday night, to be at work on Monday morning.

I'd spend the rest of the week in Lincoln Park, by myself until Friday night, and then I would make the pilgrimage to Leamington for the weekend.

Remember, I was still only sixteen! I continued through my seventeenth and eighteenth summers to live alone.

Chapter 19 - Driving into a New Life

I didn't realize how long going to night school would be. I went the school year which was from September to May. Only three nights a week and it seemed to take forever.

In September 1953 my sister Mary and her husband Jim and baby Kim flew from California to Michigan. In those days it was cheaper to fly to Michigan and drive a new car home, than it was to buy one locally.

September was the month the new cars came out. You could buy next year's model. They bought two cars. A 1954 light blue Oldsmobile "98" for Jim's parents, a 1954 red Chevrolet convertible for them.

They came to visit us where we lived, which at that time was still Victoria Avenue, Lincoln Park. We were sitting talking when Mary asked my mother how long she was going to make me go to night school. My mother wasn't too thrilled to be asked that question.

Mary came right back with "My God mom she's gonna be nineteen this year". "She" means me. Mary was right. I was a little too old to be in high school.

Mary suggested that I go home with them. I would still be old for high school, but at least I would graduate a lot sooner. Mother was not in favor of me leaving, but then why should she be?

I was working making thirty dollars a week, paying mother twenty-five for room and board to sleep on a hideaway bed couch in the living room. What a deal!

Well after talking back and forth for a long time, mother finally said "Go then!" At which point my dad said he would like to go also. Just for a vacation you understand.

Did you catch that? Daddy wanted to leave her also. Or maybe he just didn't want to be alone with her.

So that September we left Lincoln Park, Dad and Jim in the convertible; Mary, I, and almost one year old Kim in the Oldsmobile.

We would follow them and stop for lunch. Drive some more and get two motel rooms, clean up and go out for dinner. We would turn in pretty early, as Kimmy had to get to bed and they had a lot more road ahead of them.

Now you've got to remember, back then we didn't have cell phones. We didn't have

C B radios to keep in touch. Jim would keep an eye on the rear view mirror and if he didn't see us he would pull over and wait until he did. We didn't have child seats or seat belts back then. So I held Kim most of the time, except when he fell asleep, I would tuck him in on the back seat with a large towel for a nap.

Also, there were no expressways. Most of the roads were one lane each way, with a passing lane in the middle. The other roads were just two lanes.

The trip was long and hard and tiring at times. There were a few times when we would stop and "site see."

Like the time we went off track to see Bryce Canyon in Utah. We left route 66 and went north into Utah to see the famous canyon with its unique geology and beautiful colors.

I remember us following Jim out of Bryce Canyon after we had gotten back into the Olds again.

Jim pulled out first and Mary automatically followed, not looking! It wasn't until we heard an air horn of a semi-truck right behind us that almost ran into us.

Mary pulled over to the side of the road, sat there, and just shook and cried. Jim and dad turned around and came back. We all sat there for quite a while and no one saying a word.

We slowed our pace after the canyon episode. We were done "getting our kicks on route 66". We retired early that night. Mary needed some rest and some confidence building.

I couldn't drive, as I didn't have a license yet!

Chapter 20 - Sin City

The next morning we headed for Nevada. We drove through Las Vegas. We checked out the hotels and decided to stay in old Vegas.

We took a day off from traveling and spent the day in the pool at the motel. It was just a cute little Mom and Pop, but it had everything we needed. Two clean rooms and a small pool, next door to a restaurant.

After an early dinner, Mary and Jim decided we would take in the sights. My dad was tired from all the traveling and said he would stay with Kimmy, who wanted to go to bed anyway.

As I said we were in Las Vegas. It was the first time I had been there. It was the first time I had been anywhere, except for Leamington.

We walked into the casino it blew me over with all the lights, noise and bar maids with drinks walking around. My brother-in-law gave me a ten dollar bill, told me where to meet them in an hour. He said have a good time and left.

I didn't know how to do those money machines, I soon learned. Back then they paid off with silver dollars. I proceeded to put in the money. Pull the handle and collect the silver dollars.

Mary and Jim met me an hour later at the meeting spot. With me in police custody, in handcuffs, waiting for them. I wasn't old enough to bet. I didn't know what the age is now. But back then it was twenty-one.

I was only eighteen. We were told to leave and don't come back. They were nice enough to let me keep my twenty-two silver dollars. The next morning we headed toward Los Angeles. A short four to five hour drive, then we would be home at 3521 Englewood Drive Los Angeles "66".

Chapter 21 - School Days – Again

When we got back to the Los Angeles area, we had a family meeting. We all decided that dad would go to Culver City and live with my oldest sister Brenda and her family.

I would stay with my other sister Mary and her family in what was known as Los Angeles "66". I would go to Venice High School.

Venice High School had educated Myrna Loy, the famous movie star at that time. Her nude statue stood on the lawn in front of the school. The boys had a ball with that when Halloween came.

During football season our rival school would come in the night before the game and paint her red in appropriate places.

Another thing that happened at a football game was the coach drove a small V W Bug. One night all the football players lifted it onto four overturned galvanized garbage cans. Then they left it there.

After the game when everyone had gone the coach came out and saw his Bug. He had to call his wife to come and get him.

The next day after school when they had football practice, the first item of business was to take the Bug off the garbage cans. The team had a long hard practice that day.

Also in my graduating class was a guy named Sol. He was later known as

Sal Mineo who was in "Rebel without a Cause", a great movie at the time.

So it was decided that I would stay with Mary. There were times when I would go to Brenda's to stay for a while. This was after my dad left to go back to Michigan. He had stayed a few months which were possibly the happiest ones of his senior life.

I would move in with Brenda when things got a little touchy with Mary. Brenda had a daughter Bonnie, who was a couple of years younger than me. She didn't go to Venice High as she lived in the Culver City school district.

Later in September Mary took me to Venice High. It was decided that I would go into the second half of the eleventh grade, which would put me in the winter graduation class of 1955.

Back then they had two terms, A. and B. I was in the eleven B. I was nineteen in November where most of the kids were seventeen or seventeen and a half.

So I was like the old lady of the winter graduating class. It bother me a little, but I tried to fit in as well as I could.

I would go to all the football games, dances and proms, with whoever I was dating at the time. I would also go to all the senior events in my senior year. I didn't want to miss out on the senior year of my high school life, even if I was pushing twenty. I wanted to experience the whole thing.

Those kids that knew me understood. Those that didn't poked fun at me, but by this time in my life I just let it go. It was what it was!

My brother-in-law Jim had a cousin named Lenny who was a divorced man from Canada. Lenny was a brilliant scientist, who worked with Doctor Albert Einstein. Actually Lenny was a seismologist (one who studies earthquakes and their phenomena). Doctor Einstein died on April 18, nineteen fifty-five at the age of seventy six.

Doctor Einstein never took an I Q test. Some have guessed his I Q lay somewhere in between one hundred sixty to one hundred eighty. Other sources cite he might have been a idiot. Nevertheless Einstein saw things in ways people couldn't ever imagine. Something that is far better and greater than an I Q score.

Lenny would come to Mary and Jim's house almost every weekend, in his travel truck. I call it such as it was a pickup with a small aluminum house built on the bed of the truck. Lenny lived in the travel home all the time. He would pull up next to the garage and plug into the electric outlet and he was set for the week-end with a bed to sleep in. Lenny was a regular member of the family on the weekends.

Lenny would drive me over to check on my boyfriend Don, to see if he really was studying for exams, like he had told me.

Don never found out, as who would be looking for a house on wheels?

He always brought some little gadget with him from work. We always had fun trying to figure out what it was and what it was used for.

This one weekend he brought a small round soft prudish ball. As small as the ball that came with a paddle and ball game. It was amazing what it could do. The ball could bounce, curl, and stretch and best of all you could flatten it out and put it on the Sunday comics, and it would pick up the printed picture right off the page.

When you were done, you just rolled it back into a ball and the print was gone. We asked Lenny what it was and he told us it was used on the seismograph instrument (an instrument that recorded shock waves and earthquakes) rock and wiggles and move all over the place and not tear apart.

About a year later one of Lenny's colleagues put the little hunk of putty in a plastic Easter egg on the market and sold it as "Silly Putty". Needless to say he made millions.

As for Lenny, I never knew his last name. But he was sure one heck of a guy. The summer of nineteen fifty four, I worked at the Farmers Market. It was an open air market on Halifax Boulevard.

I would drive with Jim in the morning. He had a fruit and nut shop there Brenda had a yard goods shop there also. I worked at several shops that summer. Jim and I would drive back home together in the evening.

There were lots of evenings when I would baby sit for Mary and Jim. They had two little boys at this point. They ended up with three.

I slept in their den, which I'm sure put them out a lot, as Jim would use the den to do all his paperwork. I tried to be considerate, but how considerate is a teenager?

I would go with them on most of their vacations. One winter we went to the mountains. We were on a toboggan. Jim was in the back I was in the front with the boys between. Jim fell off and the toboggan went air born. I went flying and came down on my left leg and broke it. So for half of my senior year I was on crutches.

There was a sweet little Jewish guy named Harold, who offered to pick me up and take me home each day.

That was a God send as there was a large hill between our house and Venice Boulevard. It was fast going to the boulevard and really slow coming back. Normally I would walk down the hill to catch the bus for school. So needless to say I was very thankful for Harold.

He took me to a few football games and a couple of dances. The year and a half in age didn't seem to make a difference.

We went to San Diego on senior night to the amusement park, did all the things that teenagers do at a park. I rode on the merry-go-round and I caught the brass ring (which wasn't brass, just metal) I still have that in my high school scrapbook to this day.

I was dating Jack who was in the Air Force. We met though his sister Jeannie. We worked together at the local dime store, in the evening during the winter months.

Mary and I had a real falling out one winter week-end. Jack parents let me spend the night at their house with Jeannie.

When Brenda found out, she called and said I was to come and live with them. So I moved in with my niece in Bonnie's room.

My dad found out and wrote a real nice letter to Jack's parents which they thought was really nice and showed good breeding. Things calmed down and make ups were said. So I moved back to Mary and Jim's again.

Mike had always been around as you can see, weaving in and out of the picture.

Now I was in the last half of my senior year and it was getting down to the nitty gritty, getting close to graduation.

My twentieth birthday came in November. Christmas came in December. At Christmas Jack gave me an engagement ring. It was too small to it fit my finger, so he took it with him to get it sized.

We had plans to go to the beach on New Year's Eve. I had a whole week off school and almost a month to plan for graduation. I'd finally be a person, a citizen, a non-school girl and join the ranks of the working and be like everyone else and start my life. It was a long *Time Coming*

Connies graduation 1955

Graduation

Mary, John, Connie 1955

Chapter 22 - Congratulations Are In Order

New Year's didn't come off as planned. My date with Jack to see Lawrence Welk was at seven thirty that evening.

That afternoon Mike showed up with his friend Ralph, Mike was taking him back to Alameda Naval Air Station near San Francisco Bay.

Mike asked if I could go along for the ride, so he'd have company on the way back. It would only be three or four hours. I thought this would be a good time on the way back to tell Mike about Jack and me.

Now, my sister had lived in California for over twenty years. She should have known that Frisco was more than three to four hours, One Way!

As we got near Ralph's base Mike began to say things like "well maybe we should go to Frisco for New Year's Eve". I would say something like "I don't have anything to wear" as I was dressed in slacks. Mike said "well we'll buy you something."

Now think about it. It's five o'clock on New Year's Eve. We haven't even got to San Francisco yet, and we're going to dress and shoe shops? Like that's going to happen!

We let Ralph off at his base said good bye, good luck, see you. We started back toward L A-"66". You have to remember those were the days without expressways just highways with dirt sides, no C B radios, no cell phones, or texts. Oh my God what is a cell phone?

I couldn't call Jack. No phone booths on the side the road. So I decided I had better come clean and tell Mike where we stood before he got any other great ideas.

So I started to tell him that I was engaged to Jack. The ring was too small and I was getting it back tonight which the time was already past seven thirty.

With the word, "to night", Mike severed off the highway on to the dirt side and stopped the car. He slid over to my side of the front seat and said "you're not marrying him or anyone else, you're marrying me!"

He took me into his strong arms and kissed me hard. That was that! What could a girl say? He wanted to go right then and there, find a J P and get married. I still had a little sense left and said no, we should wait awhile. We pulled back on the highway and headed home. We got home after twelve. We had missed New Year's Eve, but we had one of our own.

It was officially nineteen fifty five. New Year's Day was January first. I graduated on Friday January twenty-eighth, married Mike on Sunday January thirtieth.

We went on a two day honeymoon to Miramar in El Segundo, Beautiful El Segundo where the sewer meets the sea.

We came back to Mary and Jim's house where Mike got a phone call from Port Hueneme He was to report immediately, as his unit was getting deployed to Kodiak Alaska! Goodie!, the only place in the U. S. Navy that didn't have married housing.

After three days of marriage Mike would be gone about four months. While he was gone I got a job at Pacific Bell as an information operator. Those days were long and hard. We didn't have the electronics that we have now.

We had huge books with names, addresses and phone numbers on a slanted desk. We had to leaf through them for each request. They got pretty heavy when they got past the middle of the book. We also had to plug and unplug the switch board.

But it was a job, a clean job, a good job and I liked it. It kept me busy with something to do. I made a little money while Mike was away. He was discharged on May twenty-sixth nineteen hundred fifty-five.

So here we are again, this time ready to leave for Michigan. We put my possessions in the car said goodbye to Mary and Jim. Went over Brenda's to say goodbye and as we were leaving Brenda, being Brenda, threw a whole bag of rice into our car.

It was kind of embarrassing as every time we stopped and got out of the car, the rice fell all over the ground, which looked strange to people as I was four months pregnant.

I had a few ups and downs in my young life. They seem so long ago and far away. But I had the Lord taking care of me then and I still do now.

1955 Mercury

The happy wedding day – January 30, 1955

Chapter 23 - The Long Road Back

The trip from California to Michigan was not uneventful. We were two love struck young people with our heads in the clouds. But we would soon come down to earth, with the realities of life.

People are made up of the events in their lives. Some are happy, some are sad, some are good, some are bad. But they all go into what makes a person who he or she is.

We grew up a little on that trip. Although nothing compared to the growth we would have as we lived and built our life together.

At twenty you're young and gay (happy) and you never think that everything mentally and physically won't be the same. You live in your euphoria of life thinking this would go on forever. You think the world's your oyster, than you wake up to the reality of life.

On May thirtieth we left LA 66 about three thirty in the afternoon and drove until about seven thirty that evening. We spent our first night on the road in Barstow California, at the Sands motel. It was the typical motel of the time, the car parked in front of the door of your room, which had a large window facing the parking lot.

We woke up the next morning to find that our 55 turquoise Mercury Monterey hardtop coupe had a flat tire on Mike's side.

Mike took the car to the corner gas station to get the tire fixed; I stayed at the motel to use the layover time to write postcards. We did that back then. I think the stamp was only three cents. We had breakfast while we were waiting, and left the Sands about eleven o'clock for another long drive for the day.

The next night we stayed at the Grand Canyon Inn, right on the rim of the canyon. It sounds beautiful right? It was the worst motel Ever!!

The motel employee had to sweep it out as there was so much sand on the floor. You couldn't walk in without leaving footprints. The room had two double roll away beds. Mike made a joke one for a work bench, and one to sleep on. They both squeaked. What do you expect for nine dollars a night? That was the going price for motels back then.

There was a family with children next door in the attached cabin. So it was a toss-up who made the most noise.

In the morning I woke up and Mike was gone. I looked for him and couldn't find him. His car was still there, but he was nowhere to be found. Finally he came walking along the canyon rim. I was afraid he'd fall in. he was so close to the edge.

The Grand Canyon is so beautiful. It is one of the wonders of the world. The known history of the canyon area stretches back ten thousand five hundred years. Yet no one knows how old the canyon really is. In nineteen fifty-five the Colorado River still made it's natural run through the canyon.

In nineteen sixty the Glen Canyon Dam diverted the rivers flow for power production and the irrigation of the ever expanding farming communities of the west.

The Grand Canyon is unique in the fact that it creates its own weather. Changes in the elevation have enormous impact on temperature and precipitation.

That morning we had breakfast in the Canyon Lodge. That was a nice place, made out of logs, just like the cabins.

We took some pictures, and a few last looks at the canyon said "Goodbye" to the canyon and was on our way to the Petrified

Forest, which is a United States National Park in Navajo and Apache counties in northeastern Arizona.

As we were driving to the Petrified Forest the front wheel on (Mike's side again) didn't seem right.

We got to the forest and the wind was terribly strong. It sprang the car door on my side, and slammed Mike's door completely shut. It wouldn't open. Mike had to crawl in and out of the car on my side. My door would shut but not completely, so I locked it and moved over to the middle of the front seat.

We drove about a hundred miles that day with those conditions. There were no cell phones then, and we didn't have a credit card yet! The cash was getting scarce.

We couldn't find a gas station with a mechanic on duty to do the repairs. So we kept going.

We ended up in Gallup New Mexico at the Ranchito motel late in the afternoon. We had seen an automobile repair shop when we came into Gallup. Mike woke me up at four O'clock in the morning. He wanted to make sure we would be the first in line to get the car fixed.

When he took the tire off it was hanging by only one lug nut the other four were rolling around in the wheel cover.

No wonder the tire was making those tinkling noises. We never did know if the lug nuts weren't put on tight enough back in Barstow California three days ago.

We were certainly being watched over. I guess we woke up to reality of life that day. We left Gallup around noon after a late breakfast. We had some traveling to do, and some ground to cover to catch up on our schedule. We drove four hundred and twenty-five miles that day ending up at the

Western motel in Amarillo Texas for the night.

So here we are in Texas. We had been waiting to get here. We were all set to try one of those Texas steaks we had heard so much about.

We settled into our motel. Took showers and got dressed up a little went to the nicest steak place we could find. We ordered salad, steak and fries. The steaks weren't too bad, but nothing like we had been told about the Texas Angus.

We always got pretty friendly with the waiters as we crossed the county. So we asked the waiter why the steak wasn't as good as expected. His answer really floored us. He said "Why we send our best beef out of state". "Try one in New York, Chicago, and Detroit".

After the long day we had starting at four O'clock it is needless to say we slept well that night.

We left the motel around ten O'clock the next morning. We drove a long way that day also. Along the way we ate at the iconic "Clanton's Cafe", a route 66 institution since nineteen twenty seven.

It was getting like a routine. Get up in the morning, have breakfast, stop for lunch. Hit the road again. Drive more miles than we did after breakfast.

You have to remember back in nineteen fifty-five route 66 was the long, wide ribbon that connected the west to the mid west in Chicago Illinois.

From the west it started in Palisades Park on the Santa Monica Pier. It ended at East Adams Street and North Michigan Avenue in Chicago.

Route 66 was also known as the "Will Rogers Highway", also as "Main Street of America", and "the Mother Road".

I've been on route 66 twice in my life. Once going to California and once coming back to Michigan. The last time I carried two of the most important documents of my life, my diploma from Venice High School and our marriage license. It's true you do get your kicks on route 66.

The speed limit was far less than it is today and it certainly wasn't like our expressways of today. The highway went through many large cities and small towns.

We had been on the road for five days now and it was getting exhausting, and I was in the middle of my pregnancy. But I really liked it and enjoyed the experience, and I wouldn't have given it up for the world.

In a few days we would arrive at Mike's parents' home in Michigan. We pulled into

the Venita motel in Vinita Oklahoma. This
town is the second oldest town in the state.
We got up at six O'clock that morning had
breakfast and hit the road at eight O'clock.

This was our big night tonight, the last
night on the town for a while. As we got
close to St Louis it started to rain. (Well of
course!). What would you expect?. If it's not
car trouble, it's the weather.

We got dressed for our big night and we
had a nice dinner at the Heidelberg Inn. I
asked the waiter about night clubs in the
area. He didn't know, but thought there was
one in the hotel near where he lived. We
ended up taking two waiters home. On the
way they showed us what they thought had a
night club.

When we got back to the hotel there was
a night club. There were hundreds of people
and there was no floor show. It was
supposed to be a high class club. You could
have fooled me! We finally ended up at a

quiet little bar. We had one drink and a cop came in and walked past us. That was it, as I was under age to be drinking. I was only twenty. We thought that is all we needed! To be arrested for under age drinking along with all the rest of our bad luck so far.

So we quietly got up and left. We went to a little place and had hamburgers and malts which were quite legal. We got back to our little motel around three in the morning. Thus we ended our big night on the town in St Louis.

We got up a little later the next morning and left the motel around ten. We were still a little rattled about our experience of last night, so we took our time and drove to the next town for breakfast. We were sitting in the restaurant looking at the map. Remember there was no G P S's back then, just the good old U. S. road maps.

When my dear husband discovered we had gone the wrong way. We had gone due south instead of north east.

So we put the pedal to the metal and hit the road. We were going quite fast to try to make up for the extra fifty miles we went out our way.

Just outside of Fairmount Illinois we got a speeding ticket. Now back then in the day, we had to follow the police car into town to go before the judge because we were from out of state. We had to pay up or go to jail.

This was long before they had the camera that took a picture of your license plate. Then they sent you a citation through the mail.

The brashly policeman told Mike "Follow me to the courthouse where you can pay your ticket. I'm going to Michigan next week; maybe I'll get a ticket in your state. Kind of like a payback huh?"

Yah he'd get a ticket alright. He'd just flash his shiny silver badge and speed away. So we paid our fourteen dollar ticket, said " Goodbye" to the state of Illinois, and was on our way again. That ticket took care of last night on the town money.

We were so glad to get out of that state and into Indiana. That night we stayed at the Queens Motel in Marion Indiana. We still don't like Illinois to this day. Especially since we are U of M fans and don't like the U of I crowd.

We did this whole trip on Mike's "Mustering out Pay" of six hundred sixty-six dollars and forty-eight cents. "666"! We should have been on guard from the very beginning, but we didn't know then that "666" is the mark of the beast (the anti-Christ) in the bible Rev 13:18.

Chapter 24 - Ma Mia We're Home

We got up about seven that morning. It was the last day on the road went fifty miles for breakfast as usual. But this time fifty miles the right way.

We drove toward Michigan, heading north on Indiana State highway fifteen. Ninety miles and we'd be in our own state of beautiful Michigan. We headed east taking U.S. Highway twelve or Michigan Avenue as we know it then onto U.S. Highway twenty-four or again known as Telegraph Road. We headed north to Five Mile road (Fenkell Avenue).

The trip from Indiana to home was quite nice; we went through a lot of little towns and some pretty places like Sturgis, Coldwater, and the Irish Hills to name a few.

Most interesting was passing by the famous "Willow Run Airport". It has a hangar that houses the home of "The Yankee Air Museum". It's is the largest collection of vintage aircraft in the world.

During World War 11 Ford Motor Company built the B-24 Liberator heavy bomber there. After all this driving we finally ended up at 15459 Riverdale in Detroit about one-thirty, Monday June sixth nineteen fifty-five.

Mike's mother opened the back door and looked real surprised. I didn't know if Mike didn't tell her he had gotten married, or if she just forgot. (It was probably the later). Thinking back to what she had said three years ago.

Oh Mich-cal she's not-a-Italian, she's not-a- catholic, and worst of all she's-a-English.

Welcome home Connie. So it was on my own battlefield on foreign soil. The only thing I had going for me was I was caring their first grandchild.

We lay down and rested for a while it had been a long drive. We unpacked the car. We had all my stuff, my clothes, all Mike's stuff and his uniforms and dress clothes, shoes (lots of shoes). I put all the things away, while Mike cleaned and washed the car. I put my face on (my makeup) and Mike rushed me out to go and pick up some liquor.

A little later Mike's dad came home. I was dreading that because after his mother's reception, who knew what was in store.

As it turned out Frank (Mike's dad) liked me right off the bat. He thought I was cute and knew I couldn't hold my wine.

I had met them about three years ago, when I was sampling all of dad's wine when

I fell into the dining room table. I woke up on Mike's parents' bed a few hours later.

To make things even worse Mike's mom's name is Concetta which loosely translated as Constance in English. Mike's little brother "Johnny" was thirteen then and I think he liked me too. What do you expect of a young man just entering his teens with all those raging hormones that guys have at that age?

We all sat down for dinner and talked the whole evening. Things like Mike getting a job, finding a place to live. Getting insurance for when we have the baby. It went on and on until twelve-thirty and I were getting tired and dad had to go to work the next day.

It was really hot, and they had no air conditioning. The next day we were up around ten o'clock. We were really tired from the eight day trip.

We had to go into the city of Detroit to the county building (now get this) so Mike could register for the draft. He'd already spent four years in the "U.S. Navy as a

"Sea bee" (for God's sake). We also had to go to the V.A. for something or other.

On the walk back to the car Mike put his hand in the pocket of his shirt flipping out the five dollar bill that he had just picked up at the bank when he closed his account.

We could ill afford to lose five dollars at that point in our young lives. But we were in a not so good part of the city, so we hoped that someone who needed it more than us found it.

Driving home we saw a carpenter crew at work. Mike stopped the car and walked across the field to talk to some of the men. He found out he needed to join the union first. It wasn't going to be cheap or easy getting into the "United Carpenters and Joiners of America".

While we were out, we decided we'd better get it over with and go and see my parents. Now it's Mike's turn to meet the in-laws "Turnabout is fair play" so they say.

We went to see my mother (Madam Ruth the witch) at work at the American Health Spa). "O Constance he's Italian, he's Catholic, and he's dark". Thinking back to what she had said three years ago also.

We promised to come over to the house to see them on Sunday, after a short visit with my mother, we went to the small house in Lincoln Park to see my dad (Walter). I hadn't seen him since he had left California a couple of years ago. We stayed and had an early dinner with him.

My dad was like Mike's dad. He was okay with this marriage. After we got back home, when Don a friend of Mike came over. In order to have a little privacy we went to Richard's Drive-In. I could always go for a chocolate shake. This was the place where you nosed in the car into a space, and the waitress would roller skate over and takes your order. They come back with your order on a tray and hook it to your open window of the door on the driver's side you would sit in your car and devour your burgers and shakes.

We all went to see another of their buddies, Bob wasn't home but his new wife (Louise) was. She was real cute. She and I liked each other right away. These people were the base of our friends through our married life.

It had been raining that afternoon and again that night. Then it turned really hot eighty-five degrees.

When we got home that night Mike and I sat in the car in the driveway for quite a while until midnight, then we went into our bedroom.

I tried to avoid his mother as much as possible, which was hard since we lived in the same house.

Mike's parents' house was the typical thirties house, only it was all brick. You would come into the living room from the front door. A wall divided the front bedroom (our room) from the living room walk through to the dining which was divided by a wall into the bath and a small bedroom (Johnny's room). From the dining room into the kitchen, this was divided into another bedroom (Mike's parents). At the back entrance off the kitchen were the stairs to the basement.

I was overwhelmed at the size of their house compared to the little four small room house where I had lived in Lincoln Park.

The basement of Mike's parents' house had a kitchen with a stove. Right beneath our bedroom A wine cellar that used to be a coal bin until the gas furnace came to the area. There was a wood kitchen table with a porcelain top with two sliding side panels that pulled out to make it larger. It sat in the middle of the room. Our daughter has that table in her home today.

There was a double cement laundry tub on the side wall on the driveway side. At the bottom of the stairs was a small corner room that would never become the extra bathroom. That's where we stored all our things such as wedding gifts and towels. We would go to the store and stock up on toilet paper and paper towels on sale and store them in the room for future use.

Mike did not take kindly to criticism of his mother. But every time we would go to our bedroom, she would run down stairs to cook on the stove. When I bought this to his attention, he started jumping up and down over and over again on the mattress like crazy.

I was so embarrassed at dinner that night in front of his mother who didn't like me anyway. Also in front of two people who never held hands or kissed in public, or ever kissed?

But in the years to come time has a way of changing things. We get older, we get wiser, they the grandparents get mellower and grandchildren running all over the house calm things down.

We got to the point that we hugged when we said "Goodbye" and every once and awhile there was even a kiss on the cheek.

Chapter 25 - Gotta Get- a- Job

It was raining again, or should I say "still"? We had been back three days and it had been ungodly hot or wet.

Well, today dad was home because of the weather. We drove dad over to the subdivision where he was working. Mike's dad put in those large sewer pipes that a man could walk through.

He knew the foreman of the carpenter crew. Dad had talked to him before and had told him his son had just got out of the

Sea Bees and needed a job. The guy had said "bring him over to see me".

After Mike talked to him for a little while, he sent us to the union hall. They said he had to take an exam at the "Labor

Board". That wouldn't take place until next Monday.

The carpenter foreman had told Mike to come in tomorrow to get some experience on building houses; He would start at the journeyman wage of three dollars and ten cents an hour.

So it was Mike worked for two days before going for his exam on Monday. The next morning, his first day on the job he and his dad left the house at seven-thirty. When he came home at five O'clock his hands were so calloused and he looked so tired.

We ate dinner and laid down for a while, Got up about eight, had a coke and was eating watermelon under the grape arbor in the back yard, when my mother called, and said there was a three year old house in Lincoln Park for sale.

Mike wanted nothing to do with my mother. She scared him. He couldn't quite figure her out.

That was the same evening when Mike's dad told me I was now his daughter. He had always wanted a little girl. From that day on he called me "Grasshopper" as I was always hopping around. I didn't think Mike's mother liked that too much either.

So here were two mother-in-laws that we didn't particularly like and two father-in-laws that thought it was a pretty good idea for us to be together.

Friday the last workday of the week and Mike came home just beat. On the Monday we went to the "Labor Board" where Mike took his exam. I waited in the car on pins and needles awaiting the outcome.

Mike passed his exam and we drove right over to the Redford Union Hall, number 982 to get his working card for the work quarter and also pay his dues.

That meant that Mike could now work as a carpenter. The work week would be Monday through Friday working at the regular pay scale, with Saturday and Sunday to be paid at double the regular rate. He would work every day for eight hours and leave me with his mother all day long.

Alone in second trimester of my pregnancy with a woman who didn't like me maybe even hate me, that was not a good situation.

He had made it! He was now a full fledged union carpenter with all the benefits of the union behind him. He stayed in the union going sixty-five years.

Chapter 26 - House Hunting or Haunting

The Saturday after Mike had officially became a union carpenter we went house hunting.

We left in the morning and drove through neighborhoods where we thought we would like to live. Stopping at every "For Sale" sign we saw.

We looked at some pretty sad houses. Some needed "fixing up" they were called "fixer Uppers". There were some that couldn't be fixed up. They were called "downers".

We saw a cute three year old house that we liked. They were asking fourteen thousand eight hundred for it. They came down to fourteen six but for some reason or other we didn't buy it.

That night we went bowling with our old-new gang, old to Mike and new to me. We came home around ten-thirty, tomorrow was a working day. We tried the door, we couldn't open it. Mike's mother came and opened it. She had locked us out. We sort of got the message.

Then we found a house on Bramel Street in Brightmoor, it was cute. We told them we would be back tomorrow. We looked until six O'clock, then decided to go back home for dinner. Besides I was bushed.

The next day we took dad to see the house we liked on Bramble. It was a wood sided house with two bedrooms and one bath, priced at fifteen thousand six hundred dollars. I loved it.

Dad got them down to fifteen three. There was a leak in the basement. They said the contractor would fix it and guarantee it.

We talked it over with Mike's parents. We were going to go back and buy it tomorrow. But on Monday the owner called and said we could have it as-is for fifteen six (does that mean they had decided not to fix the leak in the basement). They had gone back to their original price! So we let it go.

Mike was so mad (he gets mad a lot) that we went out and got ourselves a real estate agent.

The house that Mike's folks lived in didn't have a basement back in nineteen thirty-six when Mike and his mother came to the United States.

Dad had the house jacked up onto timbers so he could dig out the ground to have a basement built. He dug the dirt out by hand with a shovel and put the dirt in a wheelbarrow wheeled it up a ramp and dumped the dirt in the garden.

Mike's mother would rake the piles flat onto the garden. She sometimes carried pails of dirt. They both worked very hard putting in that basement.

The real estate agent suggested that we look at new houses. Homes he called them. There were several subdivisions going up at that time. The houses were about the same price we had been looking at. Besides they came with a one year warranty.

Of course we never thought of the expense of putting in a yard, shrubs and extend the existing driveway past the house for a future garage.

We went with the Realtor and started looking at houses in different subdivisions. We found a sub near Mike's folks, about two and a have miles away.

Close enough to be close and far enough to be alone. We found a house we both liked. We went back and got Mike's parents and we looked at the same house again. I really liked that particular house, but Mike's dad said to pick out one on top of the small hill in the road as sewage runs downhill. If you ever had a basement leak it could mean trouble. He should know he worked for an Italian excavator who was one of the biggest companies in Michigan at that time.

So we picked one that was practically built, but wouldn't be finished for a few weeks. This house went the depth of the lot, like Mike's parents' house, where the one I liked went the width of the lot with windows on the front.

The lots were about fifty feet wide with a double ribbon concrete drive as far as the back door of the house. We went home and sat down and talked about the house. Being that it was a new house there was no bickering about the price.

Mike's parents had told us they would lend us five or six thousand dollars for the down payment.

The price was three hundred and fifty dollars more than the house we had lost. But it held its value and through the years would increase with all the improvements we would make.

We signed the papers, put down the down payment. We picked out our colors. Now all we had to do was wait even though we were there almost every few days checking on things, reality of life again.

Chapter 27 - Fluid Drive

On Sunday we went to see my mother and dad in Lincoln Park. After dinner mother insisted that we have a cup of tea and she would read the tea leaves. Well Mike doesn't like tea. He would take a sip and shrivel up his face and shiver and shake his head (what we wouldn't do for love huh?) (It's for me).

Mother read my tea leaves and said I was going to have a boy, and he would be the first of four children. She also said I'd learn to drive and possibly buy a car soon (my mother was a charlatan). As we didn't have even two cents to rub together much less to buy a car. Mike being a skeptic told her that he's a carpenter and so he would probably fall at some point.

She then read Mike's tea leaves and told him to paint baby's room blue, as he was going to have a son. She said that we would be buying a house sooner than we thought. (Well we had already done that we just hadn't told her yet).

She also told Mike that he was going to be taking a fall at work. After we finished with the reading, we told her we had already put down a down payment on a new house. She was thrilled and said she would buy us our cooking stove, gas or electric whichever it had to be.

By the way a few weeks later Mike did fall, by backing up and falling through a fire place opening on the deck where he was working.

It was July fifteenth we were driving around in our car with the windows down as it was really hot, not raining at least. We drove past a used car lot. Mike said "I think you need to have a car so you can learn to drive before the baby gets here". We pulled into the lot; a fast talking used car salesman got us to make our first impulsive decision of our married life. (Never trust a used car salesman).

We bought a car (at least that's what the used car salesman called it). The car was a nineteen forty-eight dark blue, two door Chrysler. It had a fluid drive transmission, which meant nothing to me.

Fluid drive was the beginning of the automatic shifting. There were four forward speeds and one reverse available, first, second, third and high. Most driving is done in third or high.

You would put the gear shift in third (this would be like drive today) and it would shift into high automatically. There is no clutch pedal to push in, so no need to take the right foot off the gas pedal to push in the clutch, which was good news for me. I guess I wouldn't be dropping any more transmissions (like I had done in the good old days).

On Saturday Don drove us to pick up our new/old car. I drove it for a little while, it wasn't too bad. Later we went out for a lesson and as I went to pull out onto Fenkell putting it into what I thought was second gear, I backed up into the Oldsmobile behind me. Lucky we were at stop sign and I didn't do any damage to the Olds. I didn't have a driver's license.

On Sunday we took Johnny and Don to Kent Lake in our new/old car Mike did the driving. On Monday Mike drove it to his first union meeting. He got his Quarterly working card and his dues paying record book.

At the meeting after the business part was over they had beer and hot dogs. He had a good time. But the best part was now we had health insurance to pay for the baby. Life Is Good! (This too is a Reality of life)

Chapter 28 - Parallel Parking

We had been going out on a regular basis practicing driving; driving in the park; in parking lots, up and down driveways. Everything we could think of.

I was ready to go for my driving test and get my driver's license. There was only one thing I couldn't master, and that was parallel parking. I could not pull up to another car and back my car in the space in front or behind it I was afraid I would take off his fender or worse.

It was arranged that Don would pick me up and take me down to Detroit for my driver's test. Mike had to work and the secretary of state wasn't open on the weekend.

I told Mike's mother that Don was coming for me that morning. She said, "That didn't look good for me to drive off with Don, that the neighbors would talk".

I was upset when Don came for me. He said "Mike wants you to get your license before you get a ticket for not having one!" So we took off for the city.

I passed the question test with only one wrong. Now I was ready to take my driver's test. I got into Don's car on the driver's side, six full months pregnant, just making it behind the steering wheel. The driving instructor was sitting in the passenger's seat. I pulled out, went to the corner, and stopped, looked both ways, stuck my left arm out the window and then turned right (There were no turn signals back then). Drove in traffic for a few blocks, turned left (doing the window thing again) into a side street with on street parking. We were just about to an empty space between cars, when he was going to tell me to pull in.

I knew I couldn't do it. I was really nervous; as I got to the space he said "when do you expect your baby?" I said "It was due last week". The poor guy got all excited and said "Just keep going, turn right and head back to the office".

When I got back, Don was waiting and asked how it went. I said, "Don't ask, and just start walking". "I was legal"

When Mike got home and I told him what happened he said, "Good going girl" I told him what his mother had said, he went right down stairs and confronted his mom about who would say anything. She wouldn't commit herself.

The first sign of trouble with our new/old car Chrysler came five days later when we needed new brake pads which cost three dollars and fifty cents. Then they found we needed a part for the transmission at the cost of eighty-five dollars and twenty dollars labor fee. Two days later the brakes acted up again. We kept putting brake fluid in until we moved into our house.

Chapter 29 - Bella Casa

The day finally came. It was Wednesday August tenth nineteen fifty-five. We went downtown to sign the papers and get the keys for 9325 Virgil, Redford Township, between West Chicago and Joy Road, East of Telegraph. Close enough that Johnny could ride his bike over a couple of times a week.

Just a few weeks before we had gone to "Joe saves U dough" And bought (on payments) a two tone brown sectional couch and a two tiered corner table that was a blond Formica with black trim around the edge and black legs also two matching end tables with two turquoise matching lamps. (I now hate matching lamps). We got a bedroom set also made of Formica (They liked that back then). It was a gray dresser with six drawers three side by side with long silver handles a double bed with box springs and mattress and a gray headboard and foot board.

We got a chrome kitchen set with four chairs. Jo saves U dough threw in a small "Crosley" refrigerator as a wedding gift. We had that refrigerator in two other homes, in the basements, until the day that we sold our last home in twenty-fifteen. They made things to last back then. That fridge lasted sixty-one years and was still going when we sold it to Detroit Edison for forty dollars through their recycle program. We also sold a sixty year old freezer for fifty dollars to Edison that was still going strong.

My mother bought us a Kenmore stove from Sears and she gave us a Duncan Phyfe drop leaf table and with two matching chairs. Later we bought a cheap twelve by twelve rug from Federals for the front room, and two rugs from J.L. Hudson in

Northland, one for the dining room and one for our bedroom.

That was the extent of our furniture when we moved into our home on August the eleventh nineteen fifty-five. We moved on the fifty-eighth day after we got back to Michigan.

That morning Mike drove me to the house with rags, a pail, and a broom. The water was turned on. I had to wait for the gas and electric to be turned on while I waited for the stove and furniture to be delivered.

When Mike picked me up, the living room, kitchen and bed room had furniture. All we needed was some kind of window covering.

We drove over to the folk's house, picked up our clothes and most of our stuff out of the storage room. Packed the car full, had dinner and left.

We were going to spend the first night in our new home in our new bed with new sheets and new pillow cases and new pillows. It was such a thrill. Everything was new again including "life".

Our house sat in the middle of the second block on Virgil between West Chicago to the south, Joy Road to the north, with Telegraph Road on the west and Rouge Park Way on the east. We lived in this area of Redford Township for ten years before moving on to Plymouth Township.

I felt like I was a long way out in suburbia, away from everything. Our house was red brick with a bay window on the front (which later became the children play area). Hardwood flooring ran through the house except in the bathroom that had ceramic tile. It had a dining el in the same long room that housed the living room.

We had two bedrooms and an office or den with a French door that opened to the back yard. Later we could put in a patio or a porch on the back of the house.

But we used that room for a nursery as it was across from the master bedroom. The other bedroom would eventually become our first child's bedroom.

We continued to go over to the folks place to bring things back including our Chrysler. It didn't run and we couldn't keep it in the driveway, so we got it across the street, off the road, on the dirt in front of the cinder block basement that would eventually be another home.

The car sat there through the fall and the dirt became mud. The car sank half way up the tires. It continued to sit there through the winter and got covered with snow up to the fenders. Spring came and we had to move it. They were starting to build again, so we sold it for fifty dollars to a salvage company.

One warm spring day a wrecker came to pick up the car. The curb was too high for the wrecker to get close to the car. The cable from the winch wasn't long enough to reach. So he went over the curb with his back tire, which proceeded to sink in the mud.

Luckily for him and us, there was a bulldozer working in the neighborhood. After much pleading he came over, hooked up a chain to the wrecker, the wrecker hooked his winch to the car and they all proceeded to pull. It took a little a little doing, but soon there were three moving vehicles moving down our street toward West Chicago, leaving a trail of mud behind.

Mike's mom and dad had a friend who had passed away and their daughter didn't want her mother's wringer washer (why would she? She had a nice new washer and dryer set).

We didn't have any kind of a washing machine, so when she offered it to us, we jumped at the chance and said "thank you, thank you". You know the saying, "For free-take- to buy waste time".

On August twenty-eighth we became the proud owners of a Maytag wringer washing machine. Getting that home was a story in itself.

We drove the Mercury over to Nan's house to get the washer. Her husband unbolted the bolts on the wringer, taking it off completely. Her husband, Mike and his dad carried the washer up the stairs to the waiting car with the huge trunk large enough we hoped.

They hoisted it up and wiggled and giggled it back and forth into the trunk of the car bringing the lid down very carefully on the top of the washer tied a rope from the trunk lid to the latch. Placing the wringer in the back seat with Mike's folks and away we went.

Now getting back to 9325 Virgil was kind of a tussle we drove slowly and cars kept passing us, giving us dirty looks (what was their problem?) It was a nice sunny Sunday afternoon and we were on the typical "Sunday Drive" with a washing machine.

When we got home, I went over to Delphine's and asked if Dick could come over and give us a hand or (two).

Our neighborhood was all young couples, all expecting. All pretty much in the same boat with new homes, payments on furniture, appliances, car loans, and mortgages, and all the expenses of everyday living. All struggling to make ends meet, which they barely did at times.

Dick came over with straps, put them around the washer and the three of them slid that baby right down the stairs and into its place in the basement (that guy really knew how to get things done). I made them a "Thank You" cake later.

Dad and Mike went to the Ace hardware on Telegraph Road and purchased two aluminum clothes poles, with cross bars with four holes in them, and a long rope. They dug two holes in the back yard, mixed up some red-mix cement. They put the poles in the holes and poured the cement around them and let them dry for a few days.

Mike covered up the holes with the poles precisely in the middle and strung the rope back and forth through the holes in the cross bars. Planted grass seed and hoped that it would grow. In a couple of weeks I could use my new tool, my new benevolent washing machine.

The big day came. I never thought I'd be so excited to do the laundry I put in the hot water into the washing tub (it took a lot of water) put in the washing soap, then the pillow cases and the sheets.

The machine was right next to the laundry tub. I had the first tub filled with water for the rinse.

As I started to put the sheets through the wringer, the washing machine took off across the basement to the other side unplugging the plug and dragging the half rung and the half wet sheet from the rinse tub behind it across the basement floor. I had water and soap all over the cement floor, plus a sheet that was ten times dirtier than before I had put it in the washer.

Apparently the brake didn't work. Mike came home to an eight month pregnant historical wife crying her eyes out with a washer and a sheet on the floor on the wrong side of the basement.

He promptly went out to the backyard and picked up a couple of bricks. Picked up the sheet threw it back into the washer and pushed it back to the laundry tub and secured the washer with the bricks in front of the wheels so it wouldn't move again. From that time on I stepped gingerly over the bricks every time I washed.

The house was close enough to the folks that Johnny could ride his bike over the two and a half miles. He helped me put the clothes on the line, by carrying the basket up and down the stairs.

Our house had two features that were standard but rather unique back in the day, but would become obsolete like the washing machine.

The first one was the milk box. It was by the back door, built into the brick wall. The milkman would put the bottles of milk into the box and close the door. I would unlock the inside door and take the milk out and put it in the fridge. Each week I'd put an envelope with the "Milk Money" in the box to pay our bill. I never saw the milkman after the first time we made the contract for delivery from "Twin Pines dairy".

The other feature was the clothes chute that was in the bathroom wall behind the door. You would put your dirty clothes into the chute and they would drop to the basement floor in a heap. Sometimes the first piece landed on someone's head if they were in the right spot at the time (It's all in the timing).

The kids soon discovered they could drop their small cars and trucks and toys down the chute. I would spend hours looking for their toys, until I found them in the laundry.

These clothes chutes were popular for quite a while going into colonials and three story homes. Then they went to laundry room or utility rooms as they are known even as far as the hallway closet in the upstairs bedroom area. Today you can find a stackable washer and drier in almost any closet.

So now we were home owners along with hundreds of American newlyweds living in the suburbia. Living The American Dream.

Chapter 30 - Bundle of Joy

We started shopping for our little bundle of joy in early September. We went to Dearborn to Sam's and spent the large amount of five dollars, We got two baby blankets, eight bottles for formula, a crib sheet and four boxes of "Modes" for after the birth (that was a lot for the money).

Someone can't remember who gave us an old crib. Somewhere or other we got a four drawer chest. We painted them both white. Not pink or blue because back then we didn't know the sex of the child, like today.

I made curtains for the nursery window and door and finally made curtains for our bedroom. We needed a rug in the nursery that would have to wait for a while. We purchased a crib mattress and we had the crib sheet and a couple of crib blankets, so I guess we were ready for the big event, that was supposed to happen on October twenty-eight, which came and went without a birth.

On October thirty-first which was Halloween. I woke up with pains at three-thirty in the morning. We went to the hospital at eight O'clock, when they were five minutes apart. When we got there the pains were three minutes apart. It stayed that way on again, off again all day. Finally at four O clocks in the afternoon I asked to go home.

We went to Mike's folks house it was closer to the hospital "Mount Carmel of Detroit". I spent the evening getting up to answer the door to the sound of "Trick or Treat".

I could hardly walk back and forth with the candy for the Halloweeners, I was in so much pain. But I had come this far and I was "hell bent" on not having my baby born on Halloween. So instead he was born the day after on "All Saints Day" (what a laugh that was because he was never near to becoming a saint.

The Halloweeners had gone home and the street was quiet again. Mike's folks went to bed around eleven, the pain got worse, so we headed for the hospital around twelve. The baby didn't come that night. I had made it through Halloween Day.

So my little pumpkin could be a cute little pumpkin and not a Jack-o-Lantern. Mike stayed with me until one O'clock in the morning. He was told he had to leave (they did that back then) at four a.m. He came back at six-thirty. I was still laboring along. Finally at 8:44 in the morning our son was born I was finally finished.

I swear I would NEVER have another baby again under these conditions, you see I had been going to Mike's parents' doctor for my prenatal care. He must have been eighty years old or more. He didn't do deliveries anymore. So when I went to the hospital, I was up for grabs. I had a total stranger (hope he was a doctor) deliver my baby.

I hadn't seen him before or after. So I decided right then and there, my next child would come into this world with an Obstetrician.

I was in a room with Mike standing over me. It was over! We had a son "Michael Alan" (where did we get that name from?) I wouldn't be able to see him until later. Like I said he was born Tuesday November first, nineteen fifty-five on "All Saints Day" which it turned out he certainly wasn't ever a saint, although he was a good kid.

I stayed in the hospital for five days. Mike got two days off work that week. He brought me a dozen yellow roses (my favorite) on one day, Sanders chocolates another day (another one of my favorites).

I came home on Sunday Mike's mom had a nice dinner in the afternoon. I made Mikie's first formula that day. I went to bed that night dog tired.

Our little bundle of joy woke up six times during the night starting at nine until seven in the morning (Where are those nursery nurses that took caring of him all night?) Oh-I-guess that's- me.

During those first and second weeks, between Mike's mom and Louise, they pretty much took care of everything, except the night feedings, that seemed to come every two hours. The doctor changed his formula to 16 oz of homogenized milk, eight oz water and 2 tablespoons Karo syrup. In a few days he seemed that he was doing better. At least he was sleeping a little longer, between frequent feedings.

On November twenty-second it was a monumental day. I turned twenty-one (now I could vote) Our son was twenty-two days old (he couldn't vote) our house was eighty-four days old (It didn't want to vote). We had bought a Muntz television, blond to match the rest furniture.

Mike would take the knobs off of it, put them in his lunch pail and take them to work with him (he was a control freak). He had this idea that I sat around all day with nothing to do except watch T.V. And hold the baby. He soon found out that he was very wrong! (The knobs stayed on the T.V. Set forever).

Mike's dad's boss gave a large oval basket for Christmas. It was durable about three feet long with handles on each side. It was made out of heavy yellowish woven straw. It came with a turkey and all the fixing and other things.

After all those years of work they accumulated quite a few of these baskets. Mom used them for laundry, and put her tomato sauce canning in them in the wine cellar. They gave us one. I took that basket and put a blanket folded several times in the bottom, and put Mickie in it and threaded a light rope through the handles of the basket and put it on the back seat of the car, tied from one car door handle across to the other car door handle. Not the handles that open and close the door. The ones that you put your hand on to help you get out of the car. I would give him his pacifier and the rocking of the car would put him to sleep.

I would go with Mike to work, drop him off and have the car for the day to do grocery shopping and errands.

Now again remember we didn't have child car seats or any kind of child protection laws back then. That was left to the judgment of the parents. Some parents didn't have much sense when it came to kids and cars. Some parents still don't today, when it comes to leaving their kids in the car.

After Mikie was born, I finally got a washer and dryer set. It had been in our basement about a month, when the washer stopped running. I called the Norge corporation and they said they couldn't do anything for me unless it was a paid service call (come on a month and I have to pay for a service call).

I was furious; I called the bank who had given us the loan to buy the washer and drier. I got real dramatic and told them I had a three month old baby, diapers that were stocking up and no washing machine (they didn't have disposables, like Pampers back then) I told them I wasn't going to carry on the payments for a washer that wasn't working.

The next afternoon there was a knock at my back door there stood the Norge repair man. I learned then "The squeaky wheel gets the grease"

Someone gave us a baby swing for a gift. That gift turned out to be "mothers best friend"

I would put Mikie in it and wind up the spring and work in the kitchen. He would swing and sing (if that's what you want to call it). Mikie loved his swing. He was a swinger all his life'

Chapter 31 - "Goodbye Daddy"
(May You Rest in Peace)

Yea! I guess you guessed it from my book. I loved my dad very much. I still miss him, even to this day, which is eighty- two years since I joined his family.

It's true I was the youngest child. I never thought I was an unimportant member of the family, as far as my dad was concerned. I guess it was that I was probably home the longest. Even when I left home (not to come home single) my dad went with me when I left.

I think he was the happiest those days in California in nineteen fifty-five with his three girls. When I finally had our first son, daddy was the only one who didn't say" you should have named him this or that". Daddy was pleased that we named him after his daddy (Mike).

Dad was pretty much OK with whatever I chose to do he was always easy going. There was a time in my teen years that I thought he only loved two things, His dog "Pal" and "Me".

I knew later in life that wasn't true. He loved all his kids and maybe my mother (for saying all he put up with).

When we had Mike Jr daddy thought he was the "Cat's Meow" he was the only grandchild (on both sides) that was in Michigan. The rest of them were in California and Syracuse, New York. But none of them were little, much less babies.

So, I was special. I had given both sets of grandparents a baby boy grandchild. It was Christmas nineteen fifty-five, and we did our shopping a little early so we could manage our budget. It was Sunday December fourth and odd as it was (or was it?) I was wrapping dad's Christmas gift (a tri-fold wallet) when the phone rang.

It was my mother; she just said "your father died tonight". He had been ill. He had had Cancer which we thought was cured but, I guess it wasn't. He had turned sixty-four on February ninth.

I had six months with him before he passed away. He had a chance to see all his children happily married, also his grandchildren including the newest one, who was a month and four days old. This was the hardest chapter to write in the whole book.

Please forgive the shortness

"Goodbye Daddy"

"Love You"

Commentary from the Author

Chapter 31 and 32 were suppose to be switched, but I didn't want to end my book on such a sad note. So instead, I am going to tell you about a stunt Mike did after our son was born.

You talk about "Leaping for joy."

Well, Top This.

Chapter 32 - Written In The Wind

(Fortunes Do Come True)

My mother (the witch) had continued to read our tea leaves. (Mike never did get to where he liked tea). Almost every time she read Mike's leaves, she would tell him, "He was going to fall". It got to the point where Mike said it before she did.

Well he did little falls here and there. But nothing compared to the "acrobatic thing", he did one day when he was working by himself.

If it hadn't been for the electrician who was on the job also there would be no record of it ever happening. Certainly no one would believe Mike, if he told the story. So here it is on paper for prosperity.

This particular day Mike was alone at a "Wonderland Music Store" in Livonia. It was just being built. He usually didn't work alone. But the builder didn't want to pay for two or three carpenters. He figured one would work and the other two would watch, like the road workers. He didn't figure the job would take twice as long with only one carpenter.

But that was how he wanted it. Besides he knew that Mike was a good and fast worker. So he figured it wouldn't take that long for Mike to finish the job.

So here was Mike all by himself, had to do all the labor of putting up his ladders and scaffolding (taking a little more time than usual).

The only other tradesman in the building was an electrician, who was installing the alarm by the front door. Mike was working toward the back of the showroom off a moveable scaffold. He had to reach high, but he wasn't tall enough, so he put a six foot folding step ladder on the top of the scaffold. He still wasn't quite high enough so he took one more step to the first step next to the top of the folding ladder.

This worked out alright for a while, but he had to reach just-a little farther. He was soon airborne; as he was falling downward he reached out and garbed a bar on the scaffold he then hung there for a minute or so, then let go falling to floor and landed upright on his feet.

The electrician looked up and watched all this, (thinking he'd have to call 911). When he saw the result of the whole thing he said to Mike "Wow you are just like one of those flying Wallendas! You should sign up with them."

Now this was funny because the "Flying Wallendas" were a high wire acrobatic family that were performing with the "Shrine Circus" in Detroit that very week.

Mike didn't rush down to Detroit to get an audition with them, believe me!

Mike was always skeptical about my mother being a witch with her tea leaves and crystal ball. But that day he thought twice about it.

The funniest things about all those falls were Mike never got seriously hurt in any of them. But, he did break his arm in our second house, when he was about to paint the ceiling coming down the stairs when the bottom ladder, which was holding up the plank, which held a six foot ladder broke, and he came down ladder and all (Does this sound familiar?).

If two people have the philosophy and morality of the older years, they make things last.

The End

(No, Just The Beginning)

Epilogue

Now you've read my story

My mother was a witch

In more than one way

So you decide am I a witch?

A bitch or neither?

A personal note

I hope you enjoyed reading the book, as much as I have writing it.

The facts are true, if not unbelievable. Things are funny after they happen, Not so much at the time.

Thanks and Take care

CONSTANCE DELL

`